THE NEED FOR SALVATION

IN THE CONTEMPORARY WORLD

Everything you need to know about
salvation through Christ Jesus

**GUIDE TO DETERMINE WHETHER YOU
ARE ONCE SAVED, FOREVER SAVED, OR NOT**

FOREWORD
PASTOR CARL PALMER

THE NEED FOR
SALVATION
IN THE CONTEMPORARY WORLD

GUIDE TO DETERMINE WHETHER YOU
ARE ONCE SAVED FOREVER, OR NOT

DENNIS JK SARPONG

Dedication

I would like to dedicate this book to the New Convert classes of every church and to every soul under the heavens - especially to the middle-aged and the youth of the present generation:

Generation X – the early tech adopters.

Millennials (Gen Y) – the internet boom.

Generation Z – the digital natives, smartphones from youth.

Generation Alpha – the current children, fully immersed in AI & technology.

Generation Beta and beyond – the next Gen. deeply integrated with AI, automation, virtual and mixed realities, and other advanced technologies.

To come to the reality that, only GOD saves through Christ Jesus.

And for the men and women who stand in the gap through prayer and soul winning, serving as vessels through whom others are brought to Christ.

Contents

Endorsement

This is more than just a book—it is a heartfelt, Spirit-led message for our generation's greatest need: salvation through Christ Jesus. The author writes with clarity, passion, and biblical depth, delivering words that reaches straight to the heart.

Whether you are a believer, a pastor, or someone still searching, you will find this book both challenging and deeply encouraging—a true guide to discovering God's gift of salvation in our world today, and to understanding the critical question of whether salvation is once for all, or can be forfeited.

Rev. ET. Doku
Lead Apostle of Gospel Word Ministry

x

Acknowledgement

I would like to say thanks to a few loved ones for helping get this book published.

TEAM SARPONG

Massive thanks to my wife Millicent for your patience, prayer, precious time, editing, proofreading, and support, and to our children. Profoundly grateful for allowing me to be extremely immersed and dedicated to this beautiful project.

BEHIND THE SCENES

To Apostle Emmanuel T. Doku editor and advisor, who gave tremendous encouragement.

To Prophet Justin Afful and Prophetess Rita Asante for their prayers and allowing themselves to be a blessing to me and sharing in this vision.

And to my good friend, Sis. Linda Koranteng and family, God bless you for your relentless support.

Foreword

From the very beginning of Scripture to its final pages, the theme of salvation stands as one of the greatest needs of humanity. To be saved is to be rescued — rescued from sin, shame, and separation from God; forgiven and restored; set free to live the abundant life Jesus offers in His Kingdom here and now. In a world filled with confusion, brokenness, and longing, nothing could be more urgent or more precious.

That is why I am delighted to commend this book by my friend Dennis Sarpong. I have known Dennis for a number of years, and in that time we have journeyed together as disciples of Jesus. I have seen first-hand his hunger for God, his openness to learn, and his steady growth in faith. He writes, not from a distance, but from within that journey — as someone who is exploring, listening, and obeying. This book reflects that heart: grounded in Scripture, passionate in tone, and practical in application.

The Need for Salvation in the Contemporary World is more than a theological outline; it is a heartfelt invitation. Dennis unpacks what the Bible says about salvation, why it matters today, and how its truth transforms lives. He addresses deep questions with clarity, helping us to see not only the necessity of salvation but also the beauty of the Saviour Himself.

I recommend this book to you warmly. Read it slowly, pray as you read, and let its message stir fresh gratitude for God's grace and a renewed desire to share the Good News with others. May it deepen your own walk with Jesus and inspire you to point others towards the One who still rescues, heals, forgives, and gives life in all its fullness.

— **Pastor Carl Palmer**

'The Way'

Introduction

The 21st century presents to us an array of great technological and scientific inventions. Although some of these inventions are updated versions of older ones, today's discoveries are overwhelming. We now have technological breakthroughs for flying cars, bullet trains, and smartphones everywhere with unimaginable apps, Wi-Fi, constant communications with or without SIM cards, artificial intelligence (AI) making great impacts everywhere, GPS, self-driving cars, robots, and many more. However, despite this progress, spiritual truths remain unchanged. This book explores the need for salvation in a world full of technological wonder but spiritual longing.

Life today has become so advanced that one wonders how the future — a century from now — will look. Everything has become highly fast-paced, and many things get done within the twinkle of an eye. Due to the wide use of the internet, news and information quickly reach everyone. The world indeed has become a global village.

However, amid all these advancements, life and death remain unchanged. The aspects of human life and spirituality are constant. Science has achieved much, but life itself comes from the source—a life giver. No matter how great these inventions are, one truth stands firm: life is the most awesome, beautiful, and profound gift that man could ever receive. While these inventions are important to human existence, nothing compares to human life itself. Without life, none of these inventions would be discovered or exist. Therefore, as much as we cherish and appreciate these necessities, and our souls long for them, we should seek and appreciate the life giver above all.

It is a known fact that, regardless of how far the world advances, life ultimately comes from a source—a life giver—and the sooner we dedicate our efforts to finding this source, the better. It is with this understanding that this book was written.

Chapter 1

In A Beginning

There is a plethora of theories about the origin of mankind; however, allow me to take you through one of the oldest books ever written—the Bible. Composed over more than 1,500 years across three continents (Africa, Asia, and Europe) by more than 40 authors—some of whom wrote multiple books—the **Bible** was written in three different languages. The Old Testament was primarily written in Hebrew, with some portions in Aramaic, while the New Testament was written in Greek.

These books were not written as one piece of document by successive generations but were written by each author independently. Yet, when these writings were gathered and compiled, they complemented each other and followed a unified course, guided by the same Spirit of GOD.

To understand the need for salvation for every person under the face of the earth, we must first understand who created us, why we were created, and where we are going after the physical body dies.

The Body

Much research has affirmed the existence of a Master Creator of all things, challenging the assertions of the Big Bang theory. When we observe the perfection of creation, it becomes evident that only a perfect Being could be behind it. The body is the physical form, serving primarily as a vessel to hold the being. When a person dies, the body returns to the earth, and its function ceases. **Genesis 3:19** "*...For dust you are, and to dust you shall return.*"

The Soul

Humans are not only physical beings. Humans have souls, such that even when they are asleep, the soul remains active. We see this activity in the form of dreams. Your soul is your true representation. From a scientific or psychological standpoint, dreams are usually seen as activity in the brain's subconscious, processing emotions, memories, or stimuli which forms the definition of a soul. In **Genesis 2:7**, *"GOD breathed into his nostrils the breath of life (spirit), and man became a living being/soul."*

The term "soul" (*nephesh* in Hebrew) in this context means a living person. It is the combination of body and breath that results in life. The soul is not an entity that exists apart from the body. It is the result of the union of body and breath.

The soul is often seen as the essence of a person. It is the centre of the mind and will, encompassing emotions, intellect, and personality. In contrast, the spirit is viewed as the part that connects with GOD and is essential for spiritual life.

The soul stirs in the moment of fear, rejoices in happiness, and bears the weight of difficult decisions. Think of a day you faced a challenging situation—your soul was speaking through your doubts and emotions. **Psalm 42:11 NIV** *'Why, my soul, are you downcast? Why so disturbed within me? Put your hope in God, for I will yet* *praise him, my Savior and my God.'* This rhetorical question shows how our soul can be in conflict—an indication of the soulish aspect of human life.

> *"Behold, all souls are mine; the soul of*
> *the father as well as the soul of the son is*
> *mine: the soul who sins shall die."*
> **(Ezekiel 18:4 ESV)**

In other words, GOD is emphasizing that all humans have souls, and that the souls of men belong to Him. He who is separated from GOD through sin shall die—and the death referred to here is the second death (eternal separation from GOD).

Remember, the soul represents both the spirit and the body. While the body dies, the soul lives on. However, when tainted by sin, the soul is banished to eternal death by the righteous judgment of GOD.

The Spirit

Humans have spirits within them. This truth is recognised across nearly every religion, cult, or secret society on the face of the earth—including groups such as the Freemasons, Illuminati, Skull and Bones, Scientology, Heaven's Gate, and others.

It is important to note that many of these groups include some of the world's most prominent political leaders, business magnates, and wealthy individuals as members. These individuals often participate in making influential decisions that shape businesses, nations, and even global affairs.

Amazingly, no amount of technological advancement can produce the breath of GOD in man. The breath (spirit, life) of GOD in **Genesis 2:7** deposited in man is supernatural. The spirit of man is the very life of GOD in him. Man, therefore, is a spirit being.

The spirit is the part of you that connects directly with GOD. It seeks what is eternal and divine. As written in **Job 32:8:**

> *"But there is a spirit in man, and the breath of the Almighty gives him understanding."*

This passage reveals that the human spirit is a divine spark, enabling you to discern and understand the things of GOD. The spirit not only seeks the meaning of life, but it also operates in realms beyond the physical, reaching into spiritual dimensions that transcend ordinary human experience. Even in moments of peace, the spirit longs for deeper connection, often asking timeless questions:

- *Why am I here?*
- *What is my purpose?*
- *Where am I going from here?*

> *'For then he will return to the earth, and the spirit will return to God who gave it.'*
> ***(Ecclesiastes 12:7 -NLT)***

This emphasises that the spirit has a divine origin and destiny. Scripture indicates that the spirit in man does not perish with the decay of the physical body, but rather returns to GOD, its source. There, it is subjected to judgment, determining its final destination—whether eternal life or eternal death, and **Hebrews 9:27** NKJV says, *...it is appointed for men to die once, but after this the judgment.* This is the first death, even the death of the body.

"For the wages of sin is death, but the free gift of God is eternal life in Christ Jesus our Lord." **(Romans 6:23 ESV)**

The body of man has already been subjected to death. Once again, the death mentioned here refers to the second death, or spiritual death. However, the key point remains 'man has a spirit within him.'

In conclusion, man is a three-dimensional being—composed of body, spirit, and soul—perfectly woven together by a Great Supernatural Being, whom we call: "The LORD GOD Almighty."

Why Were You Created?

The purpose of human creation is for GOD to have a part of Himself on earth—to colonise the earth for the Kingdom of Heaven. Humans were created to take dominion, to rule, and to manage the powerful earth and everything in it that GOD has created.

> [26] *Then God said, "Let Us make man in Our image, according to Our likeness; let them have dominion over the fish of the sea, over the birds of the air, and over the*

cattle, over all the earth and over every creeping thing that creeps on the earth." [27] So God created man in His own image; in the image of God He created him; male and female He created them. **(Genesis 1:26-27)**

We see in this verse that we are created as part of GOD—in His image and likeness—not merely as random entities born from the Big Bang theory. Regardless of whether we are great or small, poor or rich, saved or unsaved, we each possess a part of GOD within us. This divine spark grants us remarkable abilities:

- *The power of imagination*
- *The power of vision*
- *The power of discovery*
- *The power of invention*

These gifts enable us to create the comforts necessary for human life on Earth. Today, we have countless examples of our creativity and innovation, such as mobile phones, ships, skyscrapers, cars, the internet, train networks, airplanes, roads, and many more.

Which of the created things, apart from humans, possesses the ability to create, invent, or manage the world?

A visit to most of the civilised world — for example, London — will further enlighten your understanding of how humans have taken dominion over the earth through the rail network systems. In London, trains run 58 meters below ground level; this remarkable fact highlights the domineering nature of mankind on Earth, fulfilling scripture.

Again, across many parts of the world, we witness amazing and profound skyscrapers, infrastructure projects, spacecraft, machines, systems, and networks that showcase achievements only humans could accomplish. This is because we were created in the image and likeness of GOD, endowed to have dominion and manage the Earth.

Gen. 1:28-30

[28] Then God blessed them, and God said to them, "Be fruitful and multiply; fill the earth and subdue it; have dominion over the fish

*of the sea, over the birds of the air, and over
every living thing that moves on the earth."*

*29 And God said, "See, I have given you
every herb that yields seed which is on the
face of all the earth, and every tree whose
fruit yields seed; to you it shall be for food.
30 Also, to every beast of the earth, to every
bird of the air, and to everything that creeps
on the earth, in which there is life, I have
given every green herb for food"; and it was
so.*

Man was created to manage the affairs of the earth;
notwithstanding, the original intent of GOD was that we
(man) may rule the earth by His Spirit in us and with Him
as the Creator. The original purpose was for man to
report back to GOD regarding the affairs of the earth.
Man was meant to rule the earth in the presence of
GOD. It was never meant for man to rule in isolation.
According to George Washington, the first United States
President, *"It is impossible to rightly govern the world
without GOD and the Bible."*

Genesis 3:8

8 And they heard the sound of
the LORD GOD walking in the garden
in the cool of the day, and Adam and his
wife hid themselves from the presence
of the LORD GOD among the trees of
the garden.

After creation, GOD remained deeply interested in the affairs of man and the Earth He had made. By descending from His glorious and marvellous throne to visit man and Earth - though there is no distance in the spirit. This is a profound event that shows how GOD cares for His creation and that man, as the head of creation was made to look up to GOD, hook up with GOD, and be accountable to GOD.

Nevertheless, man failed the simplest test of love, instructions, and obedience, and as a result, we lost our place of spiritual significance, our place of belonging, our existence in the presence of GOD, our most important family, our spiritual connectivity with GOD, and our relationship with GOD the Father.

*¹⁶ And the Lord God commanded the man, saying, "Of every tree of the garden you may freely eat; ¹⁷ but of the tree of the knowledge of good and evil you shall not eat, for in the day that you eat of it you shall surely die." **(Genesis 1:16-17)***

*⁶ So when the woman saw that the tree was good for food, that it was pleasant to the eyes, and that it was a tree desirable to make one wise, she took of its fruit and ate. She also gave to her husband with her, and he ate. **(Genesis 3:6)***

When man disobeyed GOD, shame immediately followed and wanted to hide. Ever since, human beings have been "hiding" from GOD. "*Then the eyes of both of them were opened, and they knew that they were naked; so they sewed fig leaves together and made coverings for themselves.*" — **Genesis 3:7**. Man fell from the glory of GOD and was eternally separated through disobedience (sin).

Like the prodigal son **(Luke 15:11-32)**, we lost everything that was ever important to us—that is, relationship with

GOD (he lost his place as a son, the right of a son, and the right of a family member). As a result, humanity have lost:

- *Our place as sons*
- *Our rights as heirs*
- *Our place in God's family*

The prodigal son left the Father's presence and squandered his inheritance. Similarly, we have traded relationship with GOD for independence that leads to spiritual famine.

Although humanity has taken dominion over the earth, we have lost the divine partnership, the most important aspect of the rulership, that is, ruling with GOD and by His Spirit, and for that matter, we need to go back to fulfill this mandate or the purpose of our being. Therefore, man was created to rule the earth by the Spirit of GOD and not in isolation. Ruling in isolation has resulted in chaos, greed, threats of nuclear wars, violence for wealth, human-generated pandemics - laboratory-cooked diseases, extreme poverty, wealth inequality, soaring cost of living, and much more.

The Need for Salvation

For hundreds and thousands of years, man has been searching and struggling to fill the gap of the lost glory, spiritual death, the eternal existence, and the GOD factor in many ways, such as through personal gratification, atheism, science, technology, worship of self, and worship of lesser gods, but none ever solved the problem.

In light of humanity's fall from grace and the broken relationship with GOD, salvation becomes not just a religious concept—but a divine necessity. Man's separation from GOD through sin left a void that no amount of human effort, achievement, or dominion can fill. Though we have advanced in knowledge, technology, and power, the moral and spiritual decay around us reveals that something vital is missing.

Salvation is GOD's response to our rebellion—a pathway back to Him. It is the bridge that reconnects us to our Creator, restores our identity as sons and daughters, and reestablishes our role in ruling the earth under His guidance. Without salvation, mankind continues to operate in isolation, and that isolation leads to destruction.

Salvation is not optional—it is essential for true life, purpose, and eternal destiny.

> *"Therefore, just as through one man sin entered the world, and death through sin, and thus death spread to all men, because all sinned."*
>
> *[15] But the free gift is not like the offense. For if by the one man's offense many died, much more did the grace of God and the gift by the grace of the one Man, Jesus Christ, abound to many. (**Romans 5:12 & 15**)*

The original intent of GOD for man was for the 'Garden of Eden' to be a heaven on earth and for man to live forever in communion with Him, but the side effect of disobedience (sin) is death. This is the whole story of the Bible: that through Adam's sin we inherited his identity of sin, but through Christ we are saved and have inherited His righteousness and are called the sons of GOD – *'But as many as received Him, to them He gave the right to become children of God, to those who believe in His name'* - **John 1:12.**

> *[19] In the sweat of your face you shall eat bread till you return to the ground, For out of it you were taken; For dust you are, and to dust you shall return."*
>
> *[22] Then the Lord God said, "Behold, the man has become like one of Us, to know good and evil. And now, lest he put out his hand and take also of the tree of life, and eat, and live forever"* **(*Genesis 3:19 & 22)***

If you've ever read the book of Genesis in the Old Testament, you will read about people who lived to be over 650 years old. Death was never meant for man until sin entered the heart and life of man.

Beloved, salvation through Christ Jesus our Lord is the only way that secures us back to this former glory, eternal life, belonging, GOD's family, and dominion with GOD. **John 14:6** '*Jesus said to him, "I am the way, the truth, and the life. No one comes to the Father except through Me." '*

Right there in 'Eden' when the first man sinned, GOD prepared an avenue of escape (salvation) through Christ Jesus (The Son) signifying His love and unifying us to Himself.

*And I will put enmity between the serpent and the woman, and between your offspring and hers; He will crush your head, and you will strike His heel.' (**Genesis 3:15**).*

Salvation is GOD'S free gift of eternal life through faith, based upon the finished work of Jesus Christ's sacrificial death and resurrection on the third day for all mankind (**1 Cor. 15:3-8**).

> *"For God so loved the world that He gave His only begotten Son, that whoever believes in Him should not perish but have everlasting life." (**John 3:16**)*

Why Salvation?

> *"I say to you that likewise there will be more joy in heaven over one sinner who repents than over ninety-nine just persons who need no repentance." (**Luke 15:7**)*

Salvation is of utmost important, for it is the only reason the Kingdom of GOD consistently rejoice and celebrate over the souls of men - when a soul repents and is saved. This is how precious salvation is to GOD. Indeed, salvation is the very heartbeat of GOD and the driving force that populates heaven while depopulating Hades.

If you have ever wondered why salvation, below are a few reasons:

1. To receive spiritual rebirth into the family of GOD.

> *[17] Therefore, if anyone is in Christ, he is a new creation; old things have passed away; behold, all things have become new.*
> *(2 Corinthians 5:17)*

Christ's death for sin has completely changed how GOD sees you. Instead of looking at you as a mere sinful man punishable by death, He now views those who are in Christ as righteous. *"God made Him who had no sin to be sin for us, so that in Him we might become the righteousness of God."* — **2 Corinthians 5:21**. In Christ,

GOD is not counting your sins against you but instead giving you credit for Christ's righteous life, because your spirit is reborn as a new son in Christ and your identity of wrath (sin, darkness) has been saved by grace and transformed to the Kingdom of Light.

2. Because of where you will spend eternity.

> *⁶ Yes, remember your Creator now while you are young, before the silver cord of life snaps and the golden bowl is broken. Don't wait until the water jar is smashed at the spring and the pulley is broken at the well. ⁷ For then he will return to the earth, and the spirit will return to God, who gave it. (Ecclesiastes 12:6-7 NLT)*

GOD's original design was for man to live in His presence forever walking in fellowship, free from death, shame, and separation. Adam experienced this intimate communion before the fall, and now, through Christ, GOD is re-offering that same eternal blessing. GOD never created Hades for you and has made an avenue of escape from eternal death through faith in Christ Jesus, so that if you believe in your heart and confess with your mouth that Jesus Christ is Lord, you are saved for everlasting life—**Romans 10:9-10**.

3. To reconcile with **GOD** now while you are alive.

> *18 Now all things are of God, who has reconciled us to Himself through Jesus Christ, and has given us the ministry of reconciliation, 19 that is, that God was in Christ reconciling the world to Himself, not imputing their trespasses to them, and has committed to us the word of reconciliation. (2 Corinthians 5:18-21)*

Like the prodigal son in **Luke 15:11-32**, who abandoned his family and royal identity, after some time, he realised the lost relationship, the loss of glory, sonship, and all its blessings, he came to himself and reconciled with his family and was warmly received as the son who was lost and now found.

> *17 "But when he came to himself, he said, 'How many of my father's hired servants have bread enough and to spare, and I*

perish with hunger! [18] *I will arise and go to my father, and will say to him, "Father, I have sinned against heaven and before you,* [19] *and I am no longer worthy to be called your son. Make me like one of your hired servants."'*

[20] *"And he arose and came to his father. But when he was still a great way off, his father saw him and had compassion and ran and fell on his neck and kissed him.* [21] *And the son said to him, 'Father, I have sinned against heaven and in your sight and am no longer worthy to be called your son.'*

This is the perfect situation for our reconciliation with GOD. That if you may come to yourself, understand that you cannot save yourself except GOD, and call on Him, you will be saved. Oh' lost son/daughter, come home! If we confess our sins, He is faithful and just to forgive us our sins and to cleanse us from all unrighteousness **(1 John 1:9).**

4. To take back lost glory

> *Therefore, remember from where you have fallen, and repent and do the deeds you did at first; or else I am coming to you and will remove your lampstand out of its place—unless you repent.* ***(Revelation 2:5)***

We once lived in the Garden of GOD (Eden) with constant communication and communion with GOD. We shared in the glory of GOD, and He adorned us with His mighty presence. As we fell from this grace, GOD gave us the second chance, in that whoever believes in the finished work of the cross/tree shall take back the glorious grace. And softly and tenderly Jesus is calling, calling for you and for me; see, on the portals he's waiting and watching, watching for you and for me. Come home, come home; you who are weary, come home. Earnestly, tenderly, Jesus is calling, calling. O sinner, come home! (Author: Will L. Thompson, 1880) Come home and take your place; take back your glory and position.

5. Liberation for Creation

> *"Creation waits in eager expectation for the sons of GOD to be manifested. 20. For the creation was subjected to frustration, not by its own choice, but by the will of the one who subjected it, in hope 21. That the creation itself will be liberated from its bondage to decay and brought into the glorious freedom of the children of GOD."*
> *(Romans 8:19-21)*

Beloved, the message of the cross is not only for the liberation of humanity but also tied up with all creation. As we are being saved to everlasting life, creation is also liberated from corruption into the marvellous glory of GOD, hence our liberation and manifestation as sons of GOD is crucial for the independence of creation.

In fact, many people today want to save the world in many ways, through decarbonization to sustainability, wildlife, wars, famine, and the likes. Although that's helpful, the true way is getting saved in Christ Jesus, which results in the eternal liberation of both humanity and creation.

In conclusion, Salvation is essential because it addresses humanity's deepest need, reconciliation with GOD and freedom from the consequences of sin. It offers not only the promise of eternal life but also a transformed life now rooted in grace, hope, and purpose. Ultimately, salvation is GOD's gift of love, calling us into restored relationship with Him.

GOD is not looking for superstars; He is looking for surrendered hearts.

Chapter 2

The Miracle of Salvation

Miracles are a divine signature of GOD's presence. In both the Old and New Testaments, they served as signs of His power and compassion. This chapter will explore the purpose and impact of miracles as they lead us to salvation.

Introduction

The Bible is full of inspiring stories that have changed the entire history of the world. Stories of love, redemption, courage, forgiveness, and miracles are some of the most amazing parts, although it does not appear to easily understand some of them.

Atmosphere of Miracles

There is a plethora of miracles in the Bible that go far beyond being simply jaw-dropping or amazing—they are truly awe-inspiring! Imagine standing before a vast sea or ocean and watching the waters' part, revealing dry ground beneath, giving you a clear path to walk through. This is not a scene from a movie; it's a real event recorded in the Bible. In the story of the Exodus, GOD commanded Moses: *"As for you, lift up your staff and stretch out your hand over the sea and divide it, and the sons of Israel shall go through the midst of the sea on dry land."* — ***Exodus 14:16 (NASB).***

What a miracle indeed! This act of divine intervention not only rescued the Israelites but also demonstrated GOD's supreme power and faithfulness.

Imagine attending a friend's birthday party or a grand wedding banquet. Just when the celebration is at its peak, the wine and food run out—an awkward and disappointing moment Then, a man steps forward, calmly prays over jars of water, and suddenly the water turns into the sweetest wine you've ever tasted. As if that wasn't enough, he blesses the last portion of food, and it miraculously multiplies—more than enough to feed every guest present How would you describe such an event? Incredible? Unbelievable? That's exactly what

Jesus did—turning water into wine at the wedding in Cana (**John 2:1–11**) and feeding thousands with just a few loaves and fish (**Matthew 14:13–21**). These weren't just wonders; they were purposeful signs revealing who He was and the divine power at work through Him.

How would you explain it if, in the middle of the day where you are, the sun suddenly stood still in the sky, and the moon remained fixed in its place for the entire day? In other words, imagine the Earth stopped spinning around the sun. What would that mean for you—and how would you make sense of such an extraordinary event? This is exactly what happened, as we read in **Joshua 10:13**. *'So the sun stood still, and the moon stayed in place until the nation of Israel had defeated its enemies.'* How awesome is this miracle?

We all have loved ones who have passed on and gone to be with the LORD. Now, imagine for a moment that one of those loved ones suddenly comes back to life right beside you. How lovely, amazing, unimaginable, and utterly astonishing would that be? This is exactly what Jesus did for the family of Mary and Martha. In **John 11:38-44**, He called Lazarus out from the tomb—and

Lazarus resurrected. What a powerful demonstration of Jesus' authority over life and death!

What would your life be like if you were blind today? This was the reality for Bartimaeus, a man who lived in darkness. Can you imagine the joy and gratitude he must have felt when Jesus healed him and restored his sight? The Bible is filled with many such astonishing real-life stories—miracles that reveal GOD's power and compassion, stories that continue to inspire and amaze us.

Miracles, signs, and wonders are extremely important aspects of human life and are exceedingly and exceptionally required for our daily living. You may need a miracle for a new job, for the court case, for sickness, peace, marriage, financial breakthrough, fruit of the womb, business, liberation from the powers of darkness or the powers that be, education, overseas travel, and many more. I pray that GOD answers you, that you may walk in the fullness of joy.

The Purpose of Miracles

1. Liberation from powers of darkness or the powers that be

One of the important reasons for miracles from GOD is the liberation from the powers of darkness (spiritual) or the powers that be (physical). In the story of the exodus, the Israelites were dealing with both the authoritarian powers (spiritual and physical) that had turned their freedom in living in Egypt into slavery.

> *'8 Then a new king, who did not know about Joseph, came to power over Egypt. 9 He said to his people, "Look at the Israelite people, more numerous and stronger than we are! 10 Come, let's deal wisely with them. Otherwise, they will continue to multiply, and if a war breaks out, they will ally themselves with our enemies and fight against us and leave the country." 11 So they put foremen over the Israelites to oppress them with hard labor. As a result, they built Pithom and Rameses as store cities for Pharaoh.'*
> *(Exodus 1:8-11)*

Have you ever been in a situation where your glorious days are no longer respected and your heroism is no longer rewarded? Such were the real-life circumstances of the children of Jacob—Israel; the heroism of Joseph was no longer acknowledged. The Israelites found themselves in this massive physical and spiritual bondage that made GOD unleash the ten plagues (**Exodus chapters 7 to 11**). The battle was more spiritual than we could assume it was physical. Nonetheless, the beautiful aspect of these battles and miracles of the ten plagues is right in **Exodus 9:1**: *Then the LORD said to Moses, "Go in to Pharaoh and tell him, 'Thus says the LORD GOD of the Hebrews:* **"Let My people go, that they may serve Me.**" You realised that the main purpose of the miracles of deliverance was freedom to go and worship the LORD—yes, that's the main thing. My prayer is that whatever battles you may be fighting spiritually or physically, may GOD bring you deliverance that you may go and serve Him.

2. GOD is among His People

The second important reason for miracles is that GOD shows Himself strong that He is GOD and among His people. Do you remember the popular story of David and Goliath in **1 Samuel 17?** The armies of the Israelites have lost the war even before it started. For forty days Goliath, a champion from Gath—the Philistine, came forward every morning and evening, took his stand, and defied the armies of the Israelites. All hope was lost, but suddenly, here comes a breakthrough, a teenage boy full of the anointing of GOD, who came to shift the narrative. In **verse 46** David said, *'This day the Lord will deliver you into my hands, and I'll strike you down and cut off your head. This very day I will give the carcasses of the Philistine army to the birds and the wild animals, and the whole world will know that there is a God in Israel.'* Do you see how David announced to everyone, 'There is GOD in Israel'? That is the bottom line. GOD brings miracles to everyone to announce His presence so that even in situations that seem like you are entrenched in the waters or fire, He is right there with you. My prayer is that whatever battles you may be going through right now, the presence of GOD may intervene and bring His will and His Kingdom over you and the situation. I pray for your victory in Jesus mighty name.

3. To Reveal the Will of GOD in our lives

"Beloved, I pray that you may prosper in all things and be in health, just as your soul prospers." 3 John 1:2.

This powerful verse reveals the heart of GOD and His will for each of us—that we may prosper in every way and enjoy good health, even as our soul thrives. From the beginning of creation, GOD's desire for humanity has been clear: that we would live, not die, and dwell forever in His presence. GOD's original intent was for Eden to be Heaven on Earth—a place of eternal fellowship with Him, free from sin and death. However, when the first Adam sinned, this perfect communion was broken. Yet, in His great mercy and love, GOD performed the greatest miracle of all: He sent His only begotten Son, Jesus Christ, to die for our sins and restore us to eternal life. *"For God so loved the world that He gave His only begotten Son, that whoever believes in Him should not perish but have everlasting life."* — **John 3:16**. Through Christ, we are brought back into alignment with GOD's original plan—life, prosperity, health, and eternal communion with Him. This miracle of Jesus Christ coming to replace our eternal banishment reveals to us GOD's will for our lives. That is why the scripture says, "Today when you hear His voice, don't harden your hearts as Israel did when they rebelled, when they tested Me in the wilderness. So, in my anger I took an oath: 'They will never enter My place of rest' (**Hebrews 3:7-11**).

4. Ignite and Deepen One's Faith in Christ Jesus

Have you wondered why Jesus Christ did so many miracles, signs, and wonders to the extent that a lot of them were not recorded in the Bible? As we read **John 11:42-44,** *'And I know that You always hear Me, but because of the people who are standing by I said this, that they may believe that You sent Me." 43 Then Jesus shouted, "Lazarus, come out!" 44 And the dead man came out, his hands and feet bound in graveclothes, his face wrapped in a headcloth. Jesus told them, "Unwrap him and let him go!"* Jesus reveals in verse 42 that 'we may believe.' The word believe here simply means to ignite faith in Christ, to draw the hearts of men towards GOD. In our walk with GOD, one thing we cannot do without is faith. The Bible says, 'Without faith it is impossible to please God,' (**Hebrews 11:6**). Therefore, His miracles and wonders are seeds of faith sown in us that will lead us to GOD.

5. To Demonstrate GOD's Compassion for Humanity

Another way GOD shows His care and love to us is through miraculous signs and wonders. They demonstrate His ever-present willingness to step into humanity, help, care, and transform lives. More often than not, Jesus' ministry was preceded by compassion before many miracles were performed. In **Matthew 14:14,** *'And when Jesus went out, He saw a great multitude; and He was moved with compassion for them and healed their sick.'* Compassion illustrates GOD's heart for you. **Psalm 34:18** says, *"The LORD is close to the brokenhearted and saves those who are crushed in spirit."* GOD cares for you and loves you more than anyone else could. Open up your heart and invite Jesus to take over your life.

6. To Lead us to Salvation

Miracles are like signposts directing to salvation. Miracles authenticate the message of the gospel and encourages people to get close and have a relationship with GOD. For example, Paul's encounter on the way to Damascus **(Acts 9:3-18**) and the recovery of his sight led him to salvation in Christ Jesus. The raising of Lazarus and Tabitha from death signifies that He is the life giver, and anyone who comes to him has life and more abundantly. **John 10:10.** When Jesus multiplied the five loaves of bread and two fish, it was a statement that signifies He is the bread of life, and anyone who comes to Him will never go hungry nor be thirsty **(John 6:35).** Bread/meal is essential for life, and we have heard and seen how famine around the globe has killed many. Jesus is making a phenomenal statement that 'I Am essential for your daily living both spiritual and physical —out of Me, you have life.' Everyone's life whom Jesus touched was an invitation to ignite faith that leads to eternal life. The same way today, who soever life is touched by Jesus leads to salvation.

The Greatest Miracle

Where is Brother Lazarus, whom Jesus raised from the dead? Where is Tabitha, whom Jesus raised from death (**Mark 5:41**)? Where are the lepers Jesus healed? What is the point of all these miracles? What is the essence of multiplying food and transforming water into wine? Where does the miracle of GOD lead us? Why does GOD bring us miracles?

Among the many miracles in the Bible and those GOD is doing today; one stands out as the greatest of all. It is not the kind of miracle we often feel in our physical bodies, such as the healing of cancer, tumours, arthritis, blindness, etc., nor miracles of breakthroughs. It is often said that the greatest miracle that ever existed is the miracle of salvation—in that, a sinner repents of and turns to GOD for the salvation of his/her soul. All other forms of miracles may either perish with us when we die or left behind after death. But the miracle of a repented soul—salvation through Christ Jesus—is the only one that carries on to eternal life; the only miracle in the lives of every human that lives with us after the grave.

> *'And Jesus said to him, "I tell you the truth, today you will be with me in paradise." **(Luke 23:43)**.*

This is the ultimate goal we long for. The principal reason for His death and resurrection—salvation. Salvation is the only miracle that saves the dying soul. The sinner on the cross with Jesus requested for this greatest blessing of salvation – he said 'Jesus, remember me when you come into your kingdom. He recognised the greatest need of all time – salvation of his soul. He believed unto the Messiah, and remarkably, Jesus granted his request as the physical body perishes but carries on unto eternity.

> *"For God so loved the world that He gave His only begotten Son, that whoever believes in Him should not perish but have everlasting life." **(John 3:16)***

It is only through Jesus the Christ that we are saved. **John 14:6** says, Jesus replied, "I am the way, and the truth, and the life. No one comes to the Father except through me."

The miracle of 'salvation' is the moment when heaven comes down, and glory fills your soul. It is when your sins are washed away, and your night turned into day. Salvation is a wonderful experience – one never to be forgotten. It is a day of deliverance from the powers of darkness to the Kingdom of Light. A day of divine tender compassion and intervention, and a day when you are reconnected to GOD, and His peace comes upon your soul – an experience that makes the heavens rejoice.

GOD is waiting on you with His constant miracle of salvation through Christ Jesus. Subscribe your faith with the finished work of the cross, and you will receive the instant experience of the gift of eternal life.

Chapter 3

Is Once Saved Forever Saved?

Introduction

There are approximately 2.60 billion Christians in the world today (2025); how great, joyful, and wonderful it will be to make it to heaven with the Lord.

The subject of 'heaven' is one of the major focal points in Christianity. Heaven means living an everlasting life in the spirit in the presence of the Trinity and the hosts of innumerable angels (the Kingdom of GOD). The central purpose of the death and resurrection of Jesus Christ is that we will come back home to the family of GOD and abide with Him. We as humans are privileged to be on Earth; however, we are transitioning to our everlasting home. The Earth is home but for a moment. **Hebrews 9:27** says, *'And as it is appointed for men to die once, but after this the judgment.'*

Jesus Christ told a true story of 'Heaven and Hades' in **Luke 16:19-31**. Both the rich man and Lazarus died and were buried – this tells the condition of every human on the surface of the earth, that one day we will leave our earthly home. As the story continues, the rich man found himself being in torments in Hades (a place of torment), and Lazarus was carried by the angels to Abraham's bosom.

The emphasis of this story is that there is life after death, and salvation in Christ Jesus is the guarantee to be in Abraham's bosom—heaven. Therefore, to understand whether you are saved or not is crucial to life and making choices that secure salvation through Christ Jesus our Lord.

The question "Is once saved, forever saved?" is one of the most debated topics among believers today. It sparks strong opinions on both sides, and rightly so—because at the heart of the matter lies a critical issue: eternal life. Will you make it to heaven, or could you miss it?

Some hold the view that **once you are saved— meaning, once born again—you are guaranteed**

heaven, no matter what happens afterward in your walk or relationship with Christ. According to this belief, salvation is permanent and cannot be lost. This assertion may be based on the first phase of salvation, which is justification, (see further discussion in chapter 4). Immediately when you become born-again, GOD Justifies you. Your past, present, and future sins are forgiven, and GOD declares you righteous.

Others argue the opposite: that **salvation can be lost** if a person turns away from GOD, lives in unrepentant sin, or abandons the faith altogether. According to this view, your choices and ongoing relationship with Christ matters deeply.

But instead of leaning on human opinion, let's turn to the Word of GOD. What does the Bible say about this vital question? Let's walk through the Scriptures together and allow GOD'S Word—not personal assumptions—to guide us. By the end, we'll draw a conclusion based solely on what the Bible reveals.

Salvation

Is a free pure gift of GOD based on the finished work of GOD on the cross/tree to all mankind… *and without shedding of blood there is no remission of sin (Heb. 9:22).*

Salvation is a pure gift of GOD, and no amount of works can earn it.

> *"8 God saved you by his grace when you believed. And you can't take credit for this; it is a gift from God. 9 Salvation is not a reward for the good things we have done, so none of us can boast about it."*
> *(Ephesians 2:8-9 NLT)*

In other words, **salvation** is like Noah's Ark; as long as you jump into the Ark, you are saved. The ark of salvation has already been built by GOD and not of yourself and all you need to do is to jump into it and be saved. It is a gift and not by any good deed that you should earn it.

Salvation could be likened to a father who has saved so much wealth that as long as you are born into this family, you lack nothing good; you are entitled to enjoy all the blessings of the family.

Salvation is always a gift from GOD—freely given and never earned. The moment it becomes something we try to earn, it ceases to be a gift and is reduced to a reward, or something we think we deserve.

In the same way, we are never expected to offer anything in return. To do so would diminish its value—from a priceless gift to a mere transaction or trade-off.

Guide to Determine Whether You Are Once Saved, Forever Saved, or Not

The most crucial aspect of the believer's journey with Christ is the assurance of eternal life. This section deals with identifying your right standing with GOD, which in turn translates into letting you know whether you are once saved, forever saved, or not.

The Two Perspectives

Beloved, to truly grasp whether GOD holds back His gift of salvation—or whether we can lose it by our own choices—we must examine the matter from two biblical perspectives:

1. *GOD's Perspective*
2. *The Human Perspective*

These two viewpoints offer clarity and balance. When we look at salvation solely from a human angle, we may draw conclusions based on emotions, fears, or personal experiences. But when we step back and also consider GOD'S character, His promises, and His sovereign plan, we gain a fuller understanding.

Let us explore both perspectives through the lens of Scripture, so we may rightly divide the Word of truth and come to a sound conclusion concerning this vital matter.

Perspective here simply means the capacity to view things in their truest state or to be in the right position to tell the story or situation as it is without bias or ambiguity.

1. GOD's Perspective

From GOD's point of view, salvation raises some vital questions:

- As long as it depends on GOD, will He withhold His salvation from us?
- Is His salvation for us irrevocable?
- Does He ever take back His salvation from us at a certain point in our journey with Him?

We will explore the answers to these questions in the following scriptures, as we seek to understand the true nature of GOD's salvation.

a) GOD is Dependable

GOD is reliable, and we can depend on whatever He tells or promises us. **Numbers 23:19** says, *"God is not a man, that He should lie, nor a son of man, that He should repent. Has He said it, and will He not do it? Or has He spoken, and will He not make it good?*

This verse expressly tells us that GOD's yes is yes, and no is no. His promises are sure and forever. He is not like you and me (sons of men) to lie; hence, we can trust in Him, in His Word, and in the leadings of the Holy Spirit. He is a dependable GOD, one whom we can rely on. Beloved, when men have failed you in many ways, place your trust in GOD, and He will not fail you. Just give GOD that chance, and He will prove Himself unto you.

> *'Trust in the Lord with all your heart and lean not on your own understanding; 6 in all your ways submit to him, and he will make your paths straight.' (Proverbs 3:5-6 NIV)*

b) GOD's gifts are irrevocable.

> *'For the gifts and the calling of God are irrevocable.' (Romans 11:29)*

GOD's gift and calling are constant. They are not collected back by GOD. He does not take His gift back from us. Whatever gift or calling (gift of healing, dream, prophecy, discernment of spirits, service, teaching, etc. - **Rom. 12:6-8; 1 Cor. 12:4-11**) He has deposited in you, He does not collect them; in fact, the gifts and callings are to bring us and others to His feet closer day by day.

Therefore, we can only get better with GOD. When we are born again, He justifies us—He declares us righteous based on faith in Christ Jesus and goes further to seal us with His Spirit.

> *'13 And now you Gentiles have also heard the truth, the Good News that God saves you. And when you believed in Christ, he identified you as his own by giving you the Holy Spirit, whom he promised long ago. 14 The Spirit is God's guarantee that he will give us the inheritance he promised and that he has purchased us to be his own people. He did this so we would praise and glorify him.'* **(Ephesians 1:13-14 NKJV)**

We see that as Jesus Christ promised us the Holy Spirit in **John 14:15-18**, He is delivered unto us and guarantees our inheritance in Christ and serves as a seal of our salvation. In other words, the Holy Spirit completes the work of salvation in us through faith in Christ Jesus. Hence, we can only get better with GOD. His redemption is for eternal life.

If you live by the Spirit, if the Holy Spirit leads you, your salvation is sealed in Christ Jesus – Hallelujah.

Beloved, we need to understand that in the perspective of GOD, Salvation is once saved forever saved. He does not take back His salvation or withhold it from us.

> *[16] For God so loved the world that He gave His only begotten Son, that whoever believes in Him should not perish but have everlasting life.* ***(John 3:16)***

Amazingly, the famous **John 3:16** buttresses GOD's original intent that 'whoever' means anyone from all walks of life, from anywhere, no matter the skin pigmentation, language, place of birth, nationality, culture, height or weight, rich or poor, young or old, that believes, trusts, or has faith in Jesus Christ has eternal life. We see faith in Christ Jesus as the only condition for eternal life. We see the constant love of salvation He has given unto all mankind that whoever subscribes to faith in Christ Jesus is saved. This constant of salvation of GOD is unto everlasting life.

I pray that you will subscribe your faith in Christ Jesus, and you are saved.

We can therefore conclude that GOD has made His salvation unto mankind as constant until the second coming of Jesus Christ, and His giftings and callings are without repentance; therefore, in GOD's perspective, one saved is forever saved – hallelujah.

2. Man's Perspective

Man's perspective simply means that, as long as salvation is constant and a gift from GOD, man's choices and decisions determine whether he accepts or rejects salvation and whether he accepts salvation until death, leading to eternal life or not.

> *[10] For with the heart one believes unto righteousness, and with the mouth confession is made unto salvation.*
> *(Romans 10:10)*

Beloved, in this verse, man's response to the constant gift of salvation is to believe, trust, or have faith in the finished work of the cross and confess unto salvation, and you have received eternal life. The beautiful thing in this verse is the 'heart to believe,' but the scripture says, **'So faith, or trust, or belief comes from hearing, that is, hearing the Good News about Christ—Romans 10:17.'** Amazingly, this is the work of the Holy Spirit that as we hear the Good News about Jesus, He works in our hearts, He convicts us of sin, of our standpoint to GOD's righteousness; He stirs the love of GOD in our heart; and of the judgement that awaits us, and that leads us to believe in our hearts, and confession is made unto salvation through Christ Jesus our Lord. In fact, the Holy Spirit mirrors your life in the presence of GOD's righteousness and judgment, and you immediately know your stand, which leads to trust in GOD and salvation. So even in our beliefs and confessions the Holy Spirit is right there with us, working miracles through us.

> *'And when He has come, He will convict the world of sin, and of righteousness, and of judgment.'* **(John 16:8)**

> *'For God is working in you, giving you the desire and the power to do what pleases him.'* **(Philippians 2:13 NLT)**

The Four Categories of Men

To understand man's perspective and to identify whether one is forever saved or not, we must first unfold the four categories of Men because, in reality, men do not equally have the same relationship with GOD. Each of us has different levels of relationship with GOD. Under each category, we will apply scriptures to determine whether man is forever saved or not.

To best understand these four categories of men, let's take a closer look at a parable Jesus shared about the state of four men.

The Parable of the Sower Luke 8:4-8, 11-15

> *[4] And when a great multitude had gathered, and they had come to Him from every city, He spoke by a parable: [5] "A sower went out to **sow his seed**. And as he sowed, some fell by the **wayside**; and it was trampled down, and the birds of the air devoured it. [6] Some fell on **rock**; and as soon as it sprang up, it withered away because it lacked moisture. [7] And some fell among **thorns**, and the thorns sprang up with it*

and choked it. *8* But others fell on **good ground**, sprang up, and yielded a crop a hundredfold." When He had said these things, He cried, "He who has ears to hear, let him hear!"

The Parable of the Sower Explained

11 "Now the parable is this: The seed is the word of God. *12* Those by the **wayside** are the ones who hear; then the devil comes and takes away the word out of their hearts, lest they should believe and be saved. *13* But the ones on the **rock** are those who, when they hear, receive the word with joy; and these have no root, who believe for a while and in time of temptation **fall away**. *14* Now the ones that fell among **thorns** are those who, when they have heard, go out and are **choked with cares, riches, and pleasures of life, and bring no fruit to maturity**. *15* But the ones that fell on the good ground are those who, having heard the word with a noble and good heart, keep it and bear fruit with patience.

Jesus explains the four categories of men and their state of condition in relation to the salvation of their souls. We can identify that each category of man's salvation is dependent on his choices or decisions. In the creation story, Adam made a decision that led him to fall. Our decisions determine where we will spend eternity.

The four categories of men will help you identify whether you are on the list of once saved, forever saved, or not. We shall discuss in detail the four categories of men to enable us to know our stand in Christ.

1. The Natural Man

The first man is the natural man (Mr. Natural) is one to whom the Word of GOD is preached, and this could be in many ways; it could be through one-on-one, via TikTok, radio, television, church meetings, flyers, etc., but he doubted and rejected the gospel. Jesus likened this man to one with whom the seed (word of GOD) is shared, but the devil comes and takes away lest he believe and should be saved. This person is the natural man, never being saved from the Adamic fall identity, living and ruling himself, spiritually dead, and does not recognise the need of GOD and the work of the cross. **Will this man make heaven? Is this man saved?** This man is not saved and does not have eternal life, *'for the wages of sin is death, but the gift of GOD is eternal life.' -* **Romans 6:23**.' He has never accepted the gift of eternal life. We have many uncountable people on the surface of the earth; even in your family and my family, they hear the Word of GOD but account it as foolishness and meaningless.

2. The Fallen Man

The second man, the Fallen Man (Mr Fallen), received the Word of GOD, believed, and was saved, but in the middle of the journey with Christ, he abandoned his faith due to temptations. Even now more than ever before, Christians navigate a world where faith clashes with subtle oppositions daily. Paul in **Romans 12:2** admonishes us to *'not conform to the pattern of this world but be transformed by the renewing of your mind. Then you will be able to test and approve what God's will is—his good, pleasing, and perfect will.'* Because the word of GOD has not taken deep root in the heart of the Fallen Man, he is swayed away from the feet of Christ. The

Fallen Man faces the dangers of conformity. Conformity more often than not is a series of small compromises that gradually and consistently pull us from faith. Conformity could be in the form of peer pressure or people's pressure – because everyone is doing it, let me do it so I can be accepted. Apathy towards sin—where what once was forbidden becomes acceptable, and sin becomes a norm— this can lead to spiritual decline. The Fallen Man has the tendency to easily fall into atheism and the like until his death due to conformity to the world's standards. Jesus Christ likened the Fallen Man to one who receives the word of GOD with joy but has no root in them, who believes for a while and in time of temptation falls away. **Is this man once saved, forever saved? Will this man make heaven?**

> [8] *'For by grace you have been saved through faith, and that not of yourselves; it is the gift of God,* [9] *not of works, lest anyone should boast.'*
> *(Ephesians 2:8-9)*

Beloved, among all the salvation verses in scriptures, there is a condition to salvation, and that is **'faith of**

man,' *but without faith it is impossible to please GOD* **(Hebrews 11:6).** When man's faith unites with the constant irrevocable gift (death and resurrection of Jesus Christ), it gives him salvation; likewise, the moment man abandons this same faith, he may no longer be a member of the family of GOD; he has returned to being a natural man, and he has subscribed to the Adamic nature—the fallen man.

It is extremely important to note that, **Salvation has two emblems** (Eph.2:8): the emblem of **grace** and the emblem of **faith**. Where one of these emblems is missing, salvation is incomplete. Supposing a born-again Christian forfeits, abandons, neglects, or rejects their faith in Christ and chooses instead to follow another belief system – such as a Buddhism, Hinduism, atheism, Islam, or any form of unbelieve – they cease to operate within the realms of salvation.

A typical example is Adam, he talked with GOD, had a fantastic relationship with GOD, but lost his place, his glory, his relationship, and his sonship and was eternally separated from GOD and banished from the Garden of Eden (Heaven on Earth)—**Genesis 3:22**. Adam rejected the gift and calling of GOD by his decision, choice, and disobedience and became the natural man—the fallen man. Through him today, many are in the Adamic fallen identity, an identity that displeases GOD.

A gift remains almost insignificant when it is rejected, but when it is accepted, it becomes priceless.

Where the faith of man ceases to work, GOD's sovereignty ceases to operate.

In the story of the Prodigal Son (**Luke 15:11-32),** he rejected or abandoned his family and its royal identity. And in verse *24 'for this my son was **dead** and is **alive again**; he was **lost** and is **found**.'* Jesus Christ likened the abandoning of faith or family of GOD as a one who is entirely separated (spiritually dead or lost) from all that the family represents—one who has become a natural man and forsaken the blessings of the gift of salvation. **Is this man once saved, forever saved? Will this man make heaven?** According to scriptures, I believe without doubt that this man does not have eternal life and is not once saved forever saved. He has forfeited the emblem of faith in Christ and is eternally separated from GOD.

We have heard and even witnessed real-life stories of people who once walked faithfully with Christ, but along the way their motives shifted. Some desired to perform greater miracles, gain popularity, accumulate wealth, or be celebrated by others. In pursuit of these ambitions, they eventually abandoned their faith in Christ.

> *[24] "No one can serve two masters; for either he will hate the one and love the other, or else he will be loyal to the one and despise the other. You cannot serve God and mammon. **(Matthew 6:24)***

> *[12] 'And because lawlessness will abound, the love of many will grow cold. [13] But he who endures to the end shall be saved.'* ***(Matthew 24:12-13)***

Therefore, salvation comes to those who endure to the end. In other words, hold his faith, trust, and belief in Christ to the very end.

Beloved, are you in faith with GOD? Do not let the painful experiences of life strip away from you the free gift of eternal life. In all your getting, get your salvation secured through faith in Christ Jesus.

3. The Lukewarm

The third man is the lukewarm (Mr Lukewarm), one who is saved but constantly remains in sin. This person has not abandoned his faith/trust in GOD; he still upholds Jesus Christ as his Lord and saviour, but due to the cares of the world, he is in constant sin and clings to worthless ill-gotten gains – he has a mismatched identity. He is controlled by *'all that is in the world—the lust of the flesh, the lust of the eyes, and the pride of life—this is not of the Father but is of the world'* - 1 John 2:16.

Lust is an excessive craving to gratify oneself, often to the detriment of others. Lust seeks to take as compared to love, which seeks to give. The Lukewarm is ruled by the lust of the flesh, which refers to what the body desires, fulfilling selfish desires that displease GOD, such as sexual impurity, lustful pleasures, sorcery, unforgiveness, hatred, envy, drunkenness, and the like.

Again, he may be governed by the lust of the eyes, which refers to excessive materialism—in **Genesis 3:6.**

> *'So when the woman saw that the*
> *tree was good for food, that it was pleasant*
> *to the eyes, and that it was a tree desirable*
> *to make one wise, she took of its fruit and*
> *ate. She also gave to her husband with her,*
> *and he ate.'*

The woman abandoned whatever instructions given by GOD and decided for herself, 'This I must have because it is pleasant to the eyes.' We must be careful about what we take into our eye gates. The lust of the eyes keeps us in the circles of jealousy and depression.

Also, the Lukewarm may be controlled by pride—pride here means arrogant, haughty, or disrespectful in some sense. In the verse above, she said, 'it was a tree desirable to make one wise' – that is thinking of yourself above everyone else and self-seeking no matter it cost. **Proverbs 16:18** *Pride goes before destruction, and a haughty spirit before a fall.*

Jesus had an encounter with a young rich ruler in **Matthew 19:15-30** who asked Jesus,

> *'What good deed must I do to have eternal life?" And Jesus replied, "You must not murder. You must not commit adultery. You must not steal. You must not testify falsely. Honour your father and mother. Love your neighbour as yourself.'" The young man replied, "I've obeyed all these commandments." "What else must I do?" Jesus told him, "If you want to be perfect, go and sell all your possessions and give the money to the poor, and you will have treasure in heaven. Then come, follow me." But when the young man heard this, he went away sad, for he had many possessions.*

Pride is anything we treasure more than GOD. The 'Pride of life' can refer to a strong desire for recognition or an excessive craving to be noticed. This temptation can affect anyone, regardless of their position or roles in life - whether a pastor, an architect, a prophet, a doctor, a scientist, an evangelist, a manager, or any other titles.

Many people today use good deeds as the ultimate ticket to heaven, but no amount of works without Christ can save, except faith through Christ Jesus.

Jesus likened the Lukewarm as one who, when has heard the word of GOD and is saved, goes out and is choked with cares, riches, and pleasures of life, and brings no fruit to maturity.

The lukewarm is like a man whose feet are standing on two separate paths at the same time. When those in the world are gathering, he is counted, and when those in Christ are meeting, he is numbered. He is like a jack of all trades but a master of none.

Will this man make heaven? Is this man once saved, forever saved, or not?

> [30] *'And do not grieve the Holy Spirit of God, by whom you were sealed for the day of redemption.' (Ephesians 4:30)*

We see that as sin grieves the Holy Spirit; this man is constantly grieving the Spirit of GOD. The Holy Spirit may not leave the third person yet but becomes silent due to the daily sinful life choices. As the Holy Spirit reminds and prompts him against sin, he yet brushes it off and moves on daily by his choices and decisions, which grieve the Holy Spirit until He finally may leave.

Are you spiritually alive, or are you the same old person you were before being born again? This man's deeds are as much as the fallen man's, although at the back of his mind, he upholds his faith in Christ Jesus.

Let's take a look at what Jesus is saying to this man.

> *"I am the true vine, and My Father is the vinedresser. [2] Every branch in Me that does not bear fruit He takes away; and every branch that bears fruit He prunes, that it may bear more fruit'* **(John 15:1-2)**

Jesus Christ was talking about the culture of the Kingdom of GOD. Are you bearing fruit in Christ? Are you sharing the Good News of Jesus Christ? Are you showing kindness, empathy, mercy, love, compassion, and forgiveness to others? Are you standing in the gap for others by way of prayer, soul-winning, and defending the poor and widows? Are you serving GOD? Have you presented your body as a living sacrifice, holy and acceptable as your reasonable service to GOD **(Romans 12:1)**?

I pray that you will not be cut away.

> [15] *"I know your works, that you are neither cold nor hot. I could wish you were cold or hot.* [16] *So then, because you are lukewarm and neither cold nor hot, I will vomit you out of My mouth." (Revelation 3:15-16)*

What is the essence of a tree if it does not bear fruits? Are you waiting for GOD to vomit you out, or are you already vomited out? GOD loves you and is calling you to come back, oh, backslider. Jesus said in **Revelation 3:20,** '*Behold, I stand at the door and knock. If anyone hears My voice and opens the door, I will come in to him and dine with him, and he with Me.*'

Beloved, open up your heart and accept Jesus Christ as your Lord and saviour. Allow the Holy Spirit to rekindle, revive, rejuvenate, and refresh you in the Spirit of GOD.

> [4] *Nevertheless, I have this against you, that you have left your first love.* [5] *Remember*

therefore from where you have fallen;
repent and do the first works, or else I will
come to you quickly and remove your
lampstand from its place—unless you
repent. (Revelation 2:4-5)

Another name for Mr Lukewarm is 'fallen from first love.' Do you think lukewarm people will make it to heaven when they die in their sins? It is extremely dangerous to ever think Mr. Lukewarm will make heaven—his spiritual life (salvation) is on the line of death.

4. The Spiritual Man

The fourth man is the Spiritual Man (Mr Spiritual). He is the spiritually discerned, whose life Christ reigns and is led by the Holy Spirit. He may not necessarily be a 'prayer warrior,' pastor, prophet, deacon, teacher, evangelist, or apostle, nor hold any titles in the spheres of the church, but he is a consistent believer who upholds, puts GOD first, led by the Holy Spirit, and bears the fruit of the Spirit.

Let me also emphasise here that the fourth man (Mr. Spiritual) is not one who does not sin but confesses them and repents whenever he sins and comes to himself, like **David in Ps. 51**.

Psalm 51:1-12

For the director of music. A psalm of David. When the prophet Nathan came to him after David had committed adultery with Bathsheba.

> *¹ Have mercy on me, O God, according*
> *to your unfailing love; according to*
> *your great compassion. Blot out*
> *my transgressions.*
> *² Wash away all my iniquity*
> *and cleanse me from my sin.*
>
> *³ For I know my transgressions,*
> *and my sin is always before me.*
> *⁴ Against you, you only, have I sinned*
> *and done what is evil in your sight;*
> *so you are right in your verdict and*
> *justified when you judge.*
> *⁵ Surely I was sinful at birth, sinful*
> *from the time my mother conceived me.*
> *⁶ Yet you desired faithfulness even in*
> *the womb; you taught me wisdom*
> *in that secret place.*

⁷ Cleanse me with hyssop, and I
will be clean; wash me, and I will
be whiter than snow.
⁸ Let me hear joy and gladness; let
the bones you have crushed rejoice.
⁹ Hide your face from my sins and blot
out all my iniquity.

¹⁰ Create in me a pure heart, O God,
and renew a steadfast spirit within me.
¹¹ Do not cast me from your presence
or take your Holy Spirit from me.
¹² Restore to me the joy of your
salvation and grant me a willing spirit
to sustain me. Amen.

Remember, beloved, that the spiritual man could still be the prodigal son but returns home to the family of GOD just as David the king returned to GOD in a pure heart of repentance.

¹⁷ "But when he came to himself, he said,
'How many of my father's hired servants
have bread enough and to spare, and I
perish with hunger! ¹⁸ I will arise and go to
my father, and will say to him, "Father, I
have sinned against heaven and before
you, ¹⁹ and I am no longer worthy to be
called your son. Make me like one of your

hired servants. ²⁰ *"And he arose and came to his father. But when he was still a great way off, his father saw him and had compassion and ran and fell on his neck and kissed him."* **(Luke 15:17-20)**

Jesus Christ likened the spiritual man to one having heard the word with a noble and good heart, keeping it, and bearing fruit with patience.

Will Mr Spiritual make heaven or not? Is he once saved forever saved, or not?

According to the scriptures, Mr Spiritual is definitely a sealed candidate of heaven – hallelujah!

I pray the HOLY SPIRIT inspires you to become Mr Spiritual, but if you are already – may ELOHIM bless and strengthen you in your journey with HIM through Christ Jesus our Lord.

Beloved, which of the four categories of men are you: the natural man, the fallen man, the lukewarm, or the spiritual man? Will you make heaven? A true believer cannot lose his/her salvation.

True Believers Vs. False Believers

Christians can be classified into two distinctive groups, that, is, true believers and false believers. The fact that when believers in Christ gather, many people are in the gathering does not make everyone a true follower of Jesus Christ. Similarly, neither a motorcycle nor a bicycle becomes a car overnight just because it is parked in a garage. The garage may be designed for car parking, but it is the car that fulfill the full function and purpose of that garage—not the motorcycle or bicycle. In **Matthew 7:21-23**, Jesus talks about true believers and false believers.

> [21] *"Not everyone who says to me, 'Lord, Lord,' will enter the kingdom of heaven, but the one who does the will of my Father who is in heaven. [22] On that day many will say to me, 'Lord, Lord, did we not prophesy in your name, and cast out demons in your name, and do many mighty works in your name?' [23] And then will I declare to them, 'I never knew you; depart from me, you workers of lawlessness.'*

Jesus presents the two types of people who will come to Him on "that day," that is, the day of judgment, the great day fixed by GOD that neither man nor angels know about. This day will be terrible for some and joyful for others. They are all seeking to enter the Kingdom of Heaven, but some will be rejected, and when they realise that what they believed to be their 'ticket' into Heaven is actually worthless, they will respond with complete confusion and disappointment. These are those who prophesy in the name of Jesus, which means either predicting future events or preaching doctrines in His name. They even perform miraculous acts, such as casting out demons and perhaps healing and other miracles, but all of this has no effect. Their actions are for their own glory, not His.

But who are these unfortunate people? How can they perform miracles unless it is through the power of GOD? We learn a few things about them from the text. First, we know that there are many of them. Second, they claim the name of Christ. These are not Muslims, Buddhists, or atheists. These people would gladly say, 'I am a Christian.' They do their work in the name of Jesus. They pray and heal in the name of Jesus. They preach and teach in the name of Jesus. They establish large churches and ministries in the name of Jesus. They claim to have a relationship with Him. But they are not His. In fact, He sends them away, not because He appreciates the good works they have done in His name (and many false believers have also done many good works in the name of Jesus), but because He denies all their actions and words. He has 'never' known them, and they have never truly known Him. They are not the Christians who have lost their salvation. They were never the chosen people of GOD, chosen before the foundation of the world **(Ephesians 1:4)**, separated and sanctified by the Holy Spirit **(1 Corinthians 6:11; 2 Timothy 2:21),** and justified by faith **(Ephesians 2:8-9)**. Christ harshly rebuked them, calling them evildoers, despite their outward good deeds and miracles, for they never came to Him in faith. Like the Pharisees, they knew the scriptures, scholars of scriptures, their personality embodied Christianity but had no spiritual connection with GOD. This calls for self-examination and prayer for GOD's guidance before allowing yourself to be prayed for by any prophet or pastor.

The account also emphasises the need to do the will of GOD. Are you doing the will of GOD or pursuing your own ambitions in the name of Jesus Christ?

In **Matthew 7:15-20** Jesus gives us a vivid clue on how to know false believers. *15 "Beware of false prophets, who come to you in sheep's clothing but inwardly are ravenous wolves. 16 You will recognise them by their fruits. Are grapes gathered from thornbushes, or figs from thistles? 17 So, every healthy tree bears good fruit, but the diseased tree bears bad fruit. 18 A healthy tree cannot bear bad fruit, nor can a diseased tree bear good fruit. 19 Every tree that does not bear good fruit is cut down and thrown into the fire. 20 Thus you will recognise them by their fruits.'*

In contrast, those who will enter heaven will not do so based on their miraculous achievements and accomplishments or works of any sort. They will have eternal life solely on the basis of obedience to the will of GOD (**Matthew 7:21**) — which is to believe in GOD's Son.

We need to understand that not all miracles come from GOD. In **Matthew 7:15-18**, again Jesus used two common imaginary figures to represent true believers and false believers.

In conclusion, there are two types of persons that will appear at the judgement seat of GOD. Which of them are you? To help you identify which of them you are, beloved, which of the four categories of men are you, the Natural Man, the Fallen Man, the Lukewarm, or the Spiritual Man? Will you make heaven? A true believer cannot lose his/her salvation

Prayer of Salvation

Dear LORD, I acknowledge that I am a sinner and cannot save myself. I thank you for sending unto me Jesus Christ, who died on the cross and rose on the third day to take away my sins. Jesus, I accept you as my Lord and saviour. Holy Spirit, fill my heart and life and use me for your glory. Amen.

Beloved, find a Bible-believing fellowship near you, filled with the Holy Ghost and Jesus Christ as the King, and be a member, and GOD will do great things with you.

Prayer for Loved Ones

If you are already saved by grace through faith in Christ Jesus, let us look out to our families, community, nation and pray for perishing souls.

LORD, I pray for the souls of every member of my family (mention their names) and my friends, loved ones, and neighbours (mention names) that you will have mercy on them, intervene in their situation, and save them from their sins. Let your grace of salvation abound for them and deliver them from the shackles of the enemy in Jesus mighty name… Amen.

Prayer of Gratitude for Salvation

Our Father which art in heaven, Hallowed be Thy name. Thank You for the gift of salvation – for saving me. Thank You for reaching out to me in many ways to capture my attention for Your love for me. Thank you for sending Your Spirit, the Good News, and godly people into my life, so that my journey with You may be filled with grace and become heavenly experience.

Chapter 4

The Three Phases of Salvation

Introduction

As followers of Jesus Christ, we know that salvation is a lifelong journey but not just a one-time event. We are saved, we are being saved, and we will be saved. The first step of salvation is that *'If you confess with your mouth, "Jesus is Lord," and if you believe in your heart that God raised him from the dead, you will be saved.'* **Romans 10:9** Since 'without faith it is impossible to please GOD' and to attain to the fellowship of His Son, therefore without faith no one has ever attained justification, nor will anyone obtain eternal life, but by faith that endures.

The Bible speaks of salvation in three dimensions, that is, the past, the present, and the future.

The Past—Ephesians 2:8 *'For by grace you have been saved through faith, and that not of yourselves; it is the gift of God.'*

The Present—1 Corinthians 1:18 *'For the message of the cross is foolishness to those who are perishing, but to us who are being saved it is the power of God.'*

The Future - 1 Peter 1:5 *'who are kept by the power of God through faith for salvation ready to be revealed in the last time.'*

Phases of Salvation

As we become born again, there are three phases of salvation we go through:

1. *Justification – we are saved*
2. *Sanctification—we are being saved*
3. *Glorification – we will be saved*

1. Justification (Past Salvation)

Justification is the moment GOD declares you are righteous before Him based on faith in Christ Jesus. **Romans 5:1** *'Therefore, having been justified by faith, we*

have peace with God through our Lord Jesus Christ.'
According to **Galatians 2:16** *'knowing that a man is not justified by the works of the law but by faith in Jesus Christ, even we have believed in Christ Jesus, that we might be justified by faith in Christ and not by the works of the law; for by the works of the law no flesh shall be justified.*

No amount of works can produce salvation—your good deeds cannot save you. We have heard many people say, 'I do not go to church nor have accepted Jesus as my Lord and Savior; all that matters is that I am a good person.' My friend, good works do not save one from eternal condemnation; only through faith in Christ Jesus are we saved and justified. Cornelius was an exceptional good man. In the book of **Acts chapter 10**, he was generous in charitable gifts to the poor, and he did not distribute his alms with partiality or prejudice, yet in all this, he and all his entire household accepted Jesus Christ as their Lord and saviour, and they were saved.

When we are justified through the sacrifice of Christ, there is a change from the condition in which a person was born as a child of the identity of the first Adam into a state of grace and adoption among the children of GOD through the Second Adam, Jesus Christ.

In justification, no amount of sin is weightier, extreme, huge, deep, or unimaginable; the blood of Jesus cleanses us from all unrighteousness **(1 John 1:9)**. In justification, we become holy and acceptable and pleasing to GOD. The primary purpose of justification is to honour GOD and our Lord Jesus Christ, and the secondary purpose is the right standing with GOD.

How joyful it is to understand that justification is not just a mere cleansing of sins; it is GOD's legal declaration. You are not just forgiven; you are counted righteous by faith because of the finished work of the cross by our Lord and saviour Jesus Christ.

Hebrews 11

> *' ⁵ By faith Enoch was taken from this life, so that he did not experience death.'*
>
> *' ⁷ By faith Noah, when warned about things not yet seen, in holy fear built an ark to save his family.'*
>
> *' ¹⁷ By faith Abraham, when God tested him, offered Isaac as a sacrifice. He who*

had embraced the promises was about to sacrifice his one and only son.'

' ²³ By faith Moses' parents hid him for three months after he was born, because they saw he was no ordinary child, and they were not afraid of the king's edict.'

' ²⁹ By faith the people passed through the Red Sea as on dry land; but when the Egyptians tried to do so, they were drowned.'

' ³⁰ By faith the walls of Jericho fell, after the army had marched around them for seven days.'

' ³¹ By faith the prostitute Rahab, because she welcomed the spies, was not killed with those who were disobedient.'

' ¹ Now faith is confidence in what we hope for and assurance about what we do not see. ² This is what the ancients were commended for.'

Each of these great people did or received mighty things through faith or trust in GOD. I pray that GOD gives you faith! Faith that endures, faith that conquers, faith that travails, faith that prevails, faith over all things through Christ Jesus.

I pray that faith in Christ Jesus will "move you to recognise GOD, to repent of your sins, to trust and have faith in GOD's divine mercy, and to love Him above all things; and to desire the sacraments (Baptism and Lord's Supper) and resolve to live a holy life."

What Happens at Justification?

- We are **forgiven** of all sin (past, present, and future)
- We are **declared righteous** before GOD, not by our works but by Christ's merit.
- We are **reconciled** to GOD and adopted into His family.

> *"For He made Him who knew no sin to be sin for us, that we might become the righteousness of God in Him."* **(2 Corinthians 5:21)**

2. Sanctification (Present Salvation)

Sanctification is the ongoing process of becoming more like Christ. Unlike justification, which is a one-time event, sanctification is a lifelong journey of spiritual growth and transformation. Sanctification is 'being saved.' **1 Thessalonians 4:3 NIV** *'It is God's will that you should be sanctified: that you should avoid sexual immorality.'*

Sanctification occurs after GOD justifies you, and it continues until we join Jesus Christ face-to-face, and this happens in our daily walk with GOD and the fulfilment of all righteous requirements. **Matthew 3:15-16** *15 Jesus replied, "Let it be so now; it is proper for us to do this to fulfill all righteousness." Then John consented. 16 As soon as Jesus was baptised, he went up out of the water. At that moment heaven was opened, and he saw the Spirit of God descending like a dove and alighting on him.''*

The early church believed that salvation and baptism were inseparable, although baptism itself does not save but fulfill righteous requirements, followed by the indwelling of the Holy Spirit, based on the example of Jesus' baptism and the Holy Spirit descending on Him.

How Does Sanctification Happen?

- **Through the Holy Spirit**—2 Thessalonians 2:13, *'But we are bound to give thanks to God always for you,* *brethren beloved by the Lord, because God from the beginning chose you for salvation through sanctification by the Spirit and belief in the truth.'* This indicates that salvation is initiated by God and emphasises that God has chosen believers for salvation through the sanctifying work of the Holy Spirit and our faith in Christ Jesus. **Hebrew 1:13** says, *'In Him you also trusted, after you heard the word of truth, the gospel of your salvation; in whom also, having believed, you were sealed with the Holy Spirit of promise.'* GOD has allowed the Holy Spirit to be the seal of our salvation.

- **By the Word of GOD**—John 17:17, *'Sanctify them by Your truth. Your word is truth.'* This verse highlights the importance of sanctification, which means being set apart for GOD's purposes through His truth. Jesus prayed for His followers, asking GOD to set them apart by the truth they were taught, emphasizing that GOD's Word is the ultimate source of truth and guidance for believers. This verse serves as a reminder that as believers immerse themselves in Scripture, they are transformed and prepared for GOD's work.

- **In community with other believers**—Hebrews 10:24-25—*24 And let us consider one another in order* *to stir up love and good works, ²⁵ not forsaking the assembling of ourselves together, as is the manner of some, but exhorting one another, and so much the more as you see the Day approaching.'* This underscores the importance of Christian fellowship and mutual encouragement within the faith community. It calls us to consider how we can spur one another on to love and good works, emphasizing the significance of regular gathering and exhortation.

- **Through trials and perseverance**—James 1:2 & 4 — *² My brethren, count it all joy when you fall into various trials, knowing that the testing of your faith produces patience. ⁴ But let patience have its perfect work, that you may be perfect and complete, lacking nothing.'* This is one of the important aspects of our walk with GOD. As followers of Jesus, we face many trials, challenges, and temptations, but let these produce patience, perseverance, and faith in GOD that *'being confident of this very thing, that He who has begun a good work in you will complete it until the day of Jesus Christ.' (**Philippians 1:6**)*

Many years ago, the fundamental messages of Christianity were preached everywhere. Today, the 21st

Century, these vital messages are extremely difficult to come by. They were messages that solidifies one's faith in Christ and our walk with GOD. They were messages that boost your confidence in Christ and a testament of knowing who you are in Christ.

If we understand that Sanctification is a process and within this process are the trials from GOD, the troubles and challenges of life, and temptation from the devil, then it will produce patience – an antidote to anxiety, perplexity, and fallen away from faith.

In the 'four categories of men' discussed above, in **Luke 8:4-8, 11-15,** Jesus spoke about the second category (Fallen Man) and the third category - the Lukewarm. They fell away from faith due to temptation and lust respectively. When we come to the understanding and knowledge that, in Sanctification, trials, troubles, challenges, and temptations are part of the process to get us to glorification, the better our faith will be strengthened.

The life of Jesus Christ clearly explains the process of Sanctification.

Living by the Spirit - At the beginning of His ministry, in **Luke 3:22** *'And the Holy Spirit descended in bodily form like a dove upon Him.'* We see the remarkable move of the Holy Spirit in everything He did.

By The Word - In **John 1:1,** He was the embodiment of the Word of GOD - *In the beginning was the Word, and the Word was with God, and the Word was God.'* One of His primary missions was speaking the Word that transformed many lives and it still transforming lives today.

In Community with Others - Even as GOD in the flesh, He fellowshipped in the community of His disciples and many others – He did not neglect the gathering of the Saints - **Hebrews 10:25**.

Through Trials and Perseverance - Finally, Jesus, left His throne in heaven and took upon Himself the deprave nature of man, born to the poor lowest regarded family and profession – a carpenter. He was accused, rejected, dejected, insulted, beaten, and crucified. **Isaiah 53:3** says, *"He is despised and rejected by men, a Man of sorrows and acquainted with grief. Like one from whom men hid their faces; He was despised, and we esteem Him* *not."* Yet in all these (shame, trials, temptation, and perseverance), He gazed on the glorification that was ahead. **Hebrews 12:2** says "*Looking unto Jesus, the author and finisher of our faith, who for the joy that was set before Him endured the cross, despising the shame, and has sat down at the right hand of the throne of God."*

Sanctification leads to glorification. Beloved, the pain, shame, ridicule, troubles, challenges, and temptations surrounding your life, may be signs of being in the process of sanctification. He who endures to the end shall be saved. May GOD (El-Sali) be your strength, that you may overcome the troubles of life as Jesus Christ overcame and was glorified - *I consider that our present sufferings are not worth comparing with the glory that will be revealed in us (Rom. 8:18).*

3. Glorification (Future Salvation)

Glorification is the final stage of salvation. In the journey of life, everyone looks forward to the day of glorification. When a woman is pregnant, she yearns for the day of delivery (glorification). Likewise, after a hard day work or a month long of work, we look forward to receiving our deserved rewards of payments. Similarly, in

Christianity, after our lifelong walk with Christ, we are glorified or rewarded with heaven.

Glorification is the end of salvation. Glorification occurs when believers die and they find their souls in Abraham's bosom, or when Christ comes the second time and those believers alive are caught up in the clouds to meet Christ.

> *[19]* *"There was a certain rich man who was clothed in purple and fine linen and [a]fared sumptuously every day. [20] But there was a certain beggar named Lazarus, full of sores, who was laid at his gate, [21] desiring to be fed with [b]the crumbs which fell from the rich man's table. Moreover the dogs came and licked his sores. [22] So it was that the beggar died, and was carried by the angels to Abraham's bosom. The rich man also died and was buried. [23] And being in torments in Hades, he lifted up his eyes and saw Abraham afar off, and Lazarus in his bosom.'* **(Luke 16:19-24)**

> *[24]* *"Then he cried and said, 'Father Abraham, have mercy on me, and send Lazarus that he*

may dip the tip of his finger in water and cool

my tongue; for I am tormented in this flame.'

Jesus' statement emphasises the awaiting glorification for those in Christ. At glorification, *'GOD wipes away all tears from our eyes, and there shall be no more death, neither sorrow, crying, or pain, for the old order of things has passed away.'* **(Revelation 21:4).**

The Apostle Paul writes in **1 Corinthians 15:52,** *"in a moment, in the twinkling of an eye, at the last trumpet. For the trumpet will sound, and the dead will be raised incorruptible, and we shall be changed."* Here, salvation is understood in relation to glorification—the ultimate transformation of the believer. Similarly, **1 John 3:2** declares: *"Beloved, now we are children of God; and it has not yet been revealed what we shall be, but we know that when He is revealed, we shall be like Him, for we shall see Him as He is."*

The finished product of salvation is this: we shall be like Him when He appears.

When Does Glorification Happen?

- **At death:** The soul enters the presence of the Lord—**2 Corinthians 5:8** — *'We are confident, yes, well pleased rather to be absent from the body and to be present with the Lord.'* The verse emphasises the hope and assurance that believers hold concerning eternal life. It highlights that death is not the end, but rather a transition into the presence of the LORD. This conveys a profound message about the Christian belief in life after death and the deep comfort it offers to those who have faith in Christ.

- **At the return of Christ:** Living believers will be transformed and caught up with Him - 1 Thessalonians 4:16-17 – *'For the Lord Himself will descend from heaven with a shout, with the voice of an archangel, and with the trumpet of God. And the dead in Christ will rise first. 17 Then we who are alive and remain shall be caught up together with them in the clouds to meet the Lord in the air. And thus we shall always be with the Lord.'* This describes the second coming of Jesus Christ. It states that the Lord will descend from heaven with a shout, and the dead in Christ will rise first. Following this, those who are alive and remain will be caught up together with them in the clouds to meet the Lord in the air, signifying a reunion of believers with Christ and each other. This passage offers hope and assurance of eternal life for followers of Jesus, emphasizing the importance of being prepared for Christ's return.

Key Characteristics of Glorification

- Sinless and incorruptible nature — 1 Corinthians 15:42-44
- Eternal life in GOD's presence — Revelation 21:3-4
- Perfect fellowship with Christ and all believers

Conclusion

We're justified by grace, sanctified by grace, and glorified by grace—through faith in Christ, and these three sparkling gems unite into GOD's unique gift of grace – SALVATION.

In summary, the three phases of salvation—justification, sanctification, and glorification—reveal the fullness of GOD's redemptive work in our lives. Justification declares us righteous, sanctification transforms us daily, and glorification completes our salvation when we are made perfect in His presence. Together, they show that salvation is not just a moment, but a lifelong journey and an eternal promise. AMEN.

Prayer

2 Chronicles 7:14

> *14 If my people, which are called by my name, shall humble themselves, and pray, and seek my face, and turn from their wicked ways; then will I hear from heaven, and will forgive their sin, and will heal their land.*

GOD is speaking to His people, and you are among them. Now, more than ever before, with a humble and repentant heart, we must stand in the gap and pray for the nations. Pray that the LORD will lift any heavy burdens over souls and over your nation. Pray that the LORD will forgive the sins of the nations and bless the land.

Ezekiel 18:4

> *4 Behold, all souls are mine; as the soul of the father, so also the soul of the son is mine: the soul that sinneth, it shall die.*

Intercede in prayer for the souls of your siblings, father, mother, spouse, children, uncles, aunties, friends, colleagues, neighbours, line manager, and community members - that the LORD will reveal Himself to them and bring them to the saving knowledge of Jesus Christ.

1 Timothy 2:1-4

Pray for All Men

> *²Therefore I exhort first of all that supplications, prayers, intercessions, and giving of thanks be made for all men, ² for kings and all who are in authority, that we may lead a quiet and peaceable life in all godliness and reverence. ³ For this is good and acceptable in the sight of God our Saviour, ⁴ who desires all men to be saved and to come to the knowledge of the truth.*

We pray that the mercy of GOD will overshadow the corrupt, selfish, wicked, idolatrous leadership found in nations, government, organisations, communities and councils, and family -so that all people may be saved and come to the knowledge of the truth.

We pray over systems of this world – the judicial systems, police services, parliaments, political institutions, academic institutions, pharmaceuticals, agricultural institutions, and religious bodies - that the 'Will of GOD' be established, in Jesus' name.

www.ingramcontent.com/pod-product-compliance
Lightning Source LLC
LaVergne TN
LVHW011211080426
835508LV00007B/725